Dive! Dive! Dive!

Isabel Thomas

Raintree

Chicago, Illinois

© 2007 Raintree
Published by Raintree,
a division of Reed Elsevier Inc.
Chicago, Illinois

Customer Service   888–363–4266

Visit our website at www.heinemannraintree.com

Designed by Michelle Lisseter and Bigtop
Printed and bound in China by WKT Company
Limited

11 10 09 08 07
10 9 8 7 6 5 4 3 2 1

**Library of Congress
Cataloging-in-Publication Data**
Thomas, Isabel, 1980-
  Dive! dive! / Isabel Thomas.
    p. cm. -- (Fusion)
  Includes bibliographical references and index.
  ISBN 1-4109-2588-9 (library binding-hardcover) --
ISBN 1-4109-2617-6 (pbk.)
  1. Hydrodynamics--Juvenile literature. 2.
Archimedes' principle--Juvenile literature. 3.
Submarines (Ships)--Juvenile literature. I. Title. II.
Fusion (Chicago, Ill.)
  QC151.2.T56 2006
  532'.25--dc22
                                    2006008625

13 digit ISBNs
978-1-4109-2588-6 (hardcover)
978-1-4109-2617-3 (paperback)

Acknowledgments
The publishers would like to thank the following for
permission to reproduce photographs: Corbis **pp. 12**,
25, **27**; Department of Defense **pp. 5** (Jim Brennan),
23 (PH2 August Sigur), **17**, **19**; Getty Images **pp. 6–7**
(Julian Herbert); Getty Images/PhotoDisc **pp. 20–21**,
29; Harcourt Education Limited/Tudor Photography
p. 14 (left and right).

Cover photograph of a submarine reproduced with
permission of Corbis/Steve Kaufman.
Picture research by Mica Brancic and Maria
Johannou.

Illustrations by Darren Lingard.

The publishers would like to thank Nancy Harris and
Harold Pratt for their assistance with the preparation
of this book.

Disclaimer
All the Internet addresses (URLs) given in this book
were valid at the time of going to press. However,
due to the dynamic nature of the Internet, some
addresses may have changed, or sites may have
changed or ceased to exist since publication. While
the author and publishers regret any inconvenience
this may cause readers, no responsibility for any
such changes can be accepted by either the author
or the publishers.

It is recommended that adults supervise children on
the Internet.

Contents

Some words are printed in bold, **like this**. You can find out what they mean on page 30. You can also look in the box at the bottom of the page where they first appear.

Hidden Danger

A submarine floats on the ocean. The **lookout** sailor searches all around. He spots smoke in the distance. An enemy battleship is moving toward the submarine. The only escape is to go underwater. The captain shouts the order, "*Dive! Dive! Dive!*"

Submarines are special boats. They can travel underwater. Some submarines are used to explore the oceans. They look for shipwrecks. They look for amazing sea animals.

Most submarines belong to navies. In wartime, submarines spy on enemy ships. They might try to sink the ships with guns. They also use **torpedoes**. Torpedoes are weapons. They can be fired underwater.

Submarines can float on the surface of the ocean. But they can also do something that other boats cannot. They can hide deep under the water.

lookout   sailor looking out for enemy ships
torpedo   weapon that can be fired underwater

▼ Submarines let a crew of sailors hide underwater.

5

Floating and Diving

Some submarines weigh as much as 2,500 elephants! It might seem strange that they can float. But they can float because of **forces**.

Forces are pushes or pulls. They can make objects move. They can make objects change shape.

Gravity is a force. It pulls everything toward the center of Earth. The pull of gravity gives an object its weight.

6

force   push or pull
gravity   force that pulls everything toward the center of Earth

Gravity makes things fall to the ground when you drop them. Gravity can also pull objects down through water. That is why a stone sinks when you drop it into a pond. But some objects do not sink.

When something is in water, it pushes some of the water out of its way. The water pushes back! Try pushing a beach ball underwater. You can feel the water pushing back.

▼Gravity pulls the submarine downward. The water pushes it upward.

How hard does the water push back?

Water has a pushing **force**. It pushes up on everything in it. This is called a **buoyant force**. It pushes a submarine upward.

Weight is the force caused by **gravity**. Weight pulls the submarine downward.

- The submarine will rise if the buoyant force is greater than its weight.

- The submarine will float if the buoyant force is exactly the same as its weight.

- The submarine will sink if the buoyant force is less than its weight.

The size of the buoyant force is different for every object. It depends on the amount of water that the object pushes out of its way.

Super strong

The buoyant force makes it easy to lift a person in a swimming pool. Weight pulls the person downward. The buoyant force pushes him or her upward. It cancels out some of the person's weight.

buoyant force force that pushes an object upward when it is in water

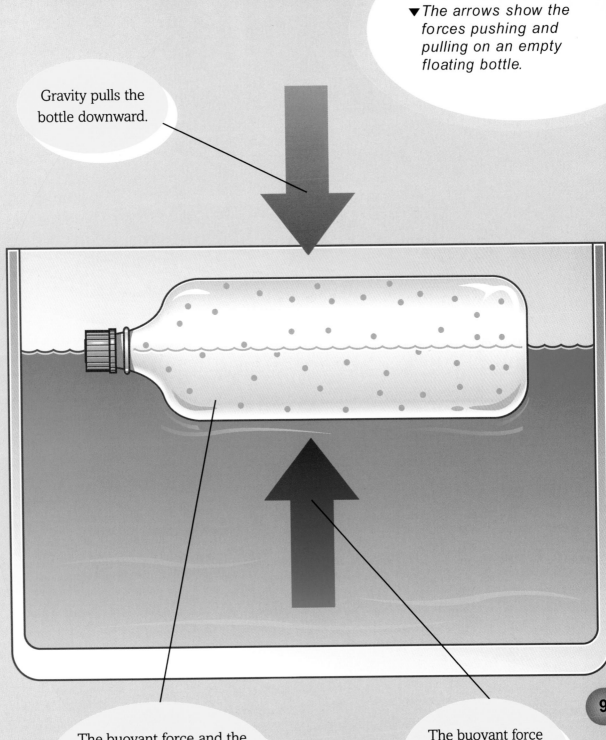

The arrows show the forces pushing and pulling on an empty floating bottle.

Gravity pulls the bottle downward.

The buoyant force and the bottle's weight are the same size. They cancel each other out. The bottle floats.

The buoyant force of the water pushes the bottle upward.

Objects that are denser ▼
than water will sink.
Objects less dense than
water will float. Objects
that are the same density
as water will float, too.

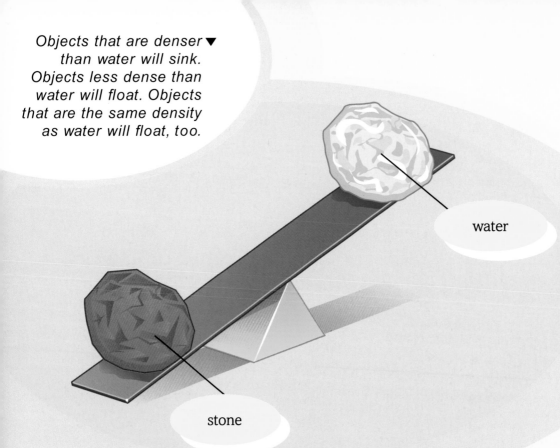

water

stone

A hollow submarine ▼
weighs the same as the
submarine-sized
amount of water.
It floats.

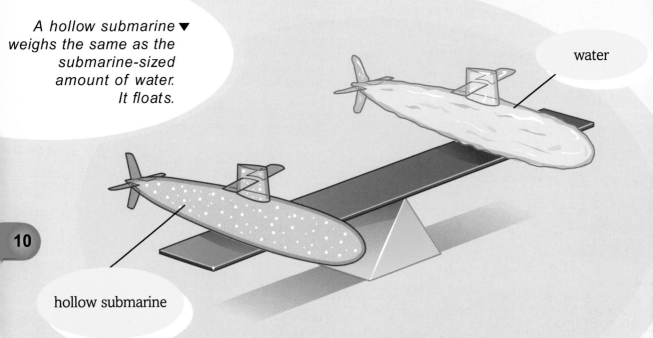

water

hollow submarine

Making metal float

Weight pulls an object downward. The object will only float if the **buoyant force** cancels out the weight.

The upward push of water is greater if more water is **displaced**. Displaced means moved out of the way. A stone displaces a stone-sized amount of water. A submarine displaces a submarine-sized amount of water. The buoyant force on a submarine is greater than the **force** on a stone.

The **density** of the object is important. Density is how heavy an object is for its size. It is the **mass** of an object divided by its size. Mass is how much there is of an object. Metal is denser than water. Solid metal weighs more than the water it displaces. It sinks.

A submarine is made of metal. But it can float. This is because it is **hollow**. There is an empty space inside. This makes it bigger than the same mass of solid metal. It displaces more water. The buoyant force is much greater.

density	mass of an object divided by its size
displace	move out of the way
hollow	has an empty space inside
mass	how much there is of an object

Dive! Dive! Dive!

Submarines have big **ballast tanks**. If the ballast tanks are empty, the submarine is less **dense** than water. It is less heavy for its size. It floats.

To dive, the submarine must get heavier. Its weight must increase to pull it down through the water. Its weight must become greater than the **buoyant force** pushing it upward.

To dive, a ▼ submarine needs to become heavier than the water it displaces.

ballast tanks big tanks inside a submarine that can be empty or full of water

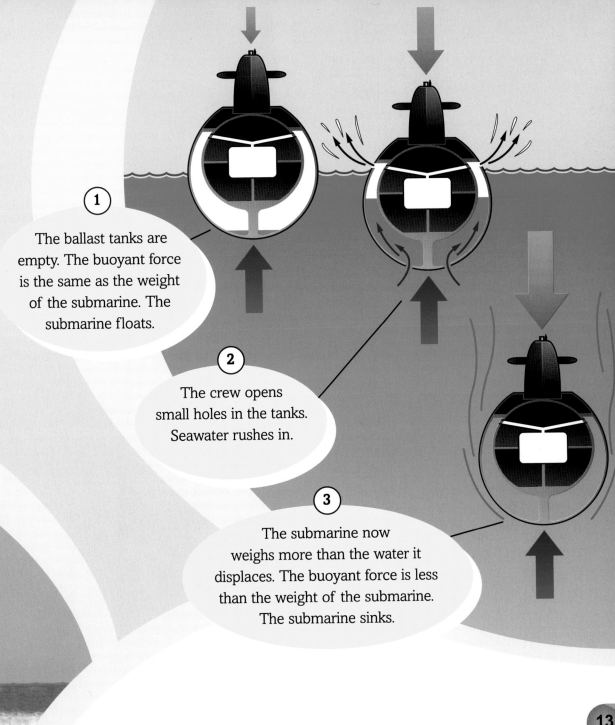

1. The ballast tanks are empty. The buoyant force is the same as the weight of the submarine. The submarine floats.

2. The crew opens small holes in the tanks. Seawater rushes in.

3. The submarine now weighs more than the water it displaces. The buoyant force is less than the weight of the submarine. The submarine sinks.

To dive, the crew fills the ballast tanks with water. The density of the submarine is now greater. The submarine is heavier than the water it **displaces**. The submarine sinks.

Water Force

Water pushes on a diving submarine from all directions. Deep in the ocean, the **force** of water is enormous.

Try crushing an air-filled plastic bottle. It is easy because the plastic is not strong. The force of your hands can crush the air into a smaller space. But you cannot squeeze the air inside a glass bottle. The glass is much stronger than plastic.

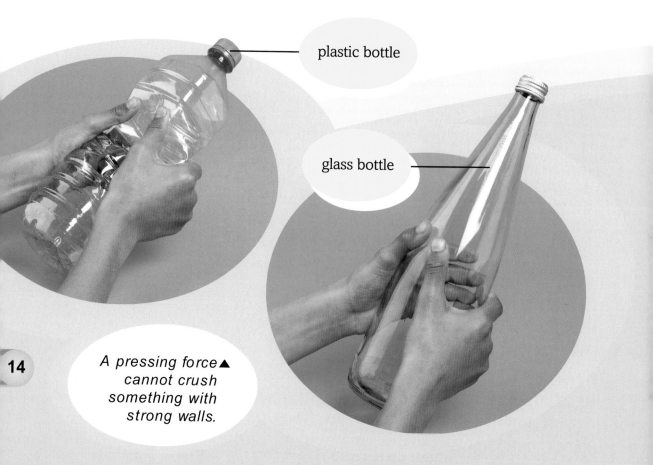

plastic bottle

glass bottle

A pressing force▲ cannot crush something with strong walls.

hull   metal body of a submarine

Water presses hard on the walls of a submarine. Submarines have very strong walls. They stop the force of the water outside from squeezing the air inside.

The body of a submarine is called the **hull**. It has two layers. The first layer is the outer hull. The second layer is the inner hull. The crew lives and works in the inner hull. The inner hull protects the crew. It protects the air that the crew breathes. It stops the crew members from being crushed by the force of the water outside.

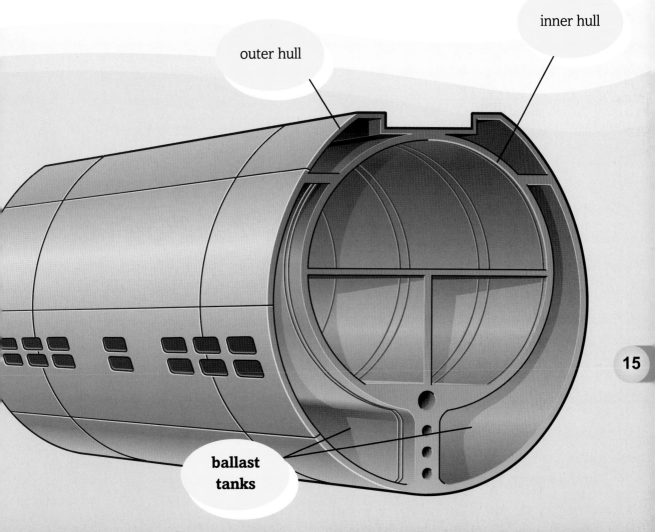

inner hull

outer hull

ballast tanks

On the Move

Most submarines are powered by **diesel engines**. They burn diesel **fuel** to release energy. The energy turns the **propeller**. The propeller has blades that spin around. It pushes the submarine through the water.

Diesel needs air to burn. The diesel engines are turned off when the submarine dives. The air on board must be saved. The crew members need the air to breathe.

An **electric engine** is used underwater. Giant batteries store electricity. Electricity is used to turn the propeller. It is used to light and heat the submarine.

The diesel engine is switched back on when the submarine comes to the surface. It recharges the batteries for the next dive.

diesel engine	machine that burns diesel fuel to release energy
electric engine	machine that releases energy from electricity
fuel	anything that is burned to release energy
propeller	spinning blades that push a submarine through water

In the 1940s, recharging a submarine's batteries was dangerous. The submarine could be spotted on the surface by enemy ships.

Coming up again

A diesel submarine can only stay underwater until its batteries run out. Then, it comes up to the surface. It runs the **diesel engine**. The diesel engine recharges the batteries.

To dive, submarines must fill their **ballast tanks** with water. To rise up, the crew has to get water *out* of the ballast tanks. Submarines carry tanks of **compressed** air. The air has been crushed. It takes up less space than normal.

The air is blown into the ballast tanks. It **expands**. This means that the air spreads out. It fills more space. It fills the tanks. It pushes the water out of the tanks. The submarine gets lighter.

Weight still pulls the submarine down. But the weight is now less than the **buoyant force**. The buoyant force pushes the submarine up to the surface.

Submarines can ▶ rise so fast that the nose shoots out of the water.

compressed	crushed into a small space
expand	spread out to fill more space

Steering in four directions

Like all boats, submarines have a **rudder**. This is a large blade. It is at the back of the submarine. A wheel in the control room turns the rudder. This steers the submarine left or right.

Submarines also have four small "wings." The wings are called hydroplanes. The crew members move the hydroplanes to tilt the nose. They move the nose of the submarine up or down. This helps the submarine to rise or sink.

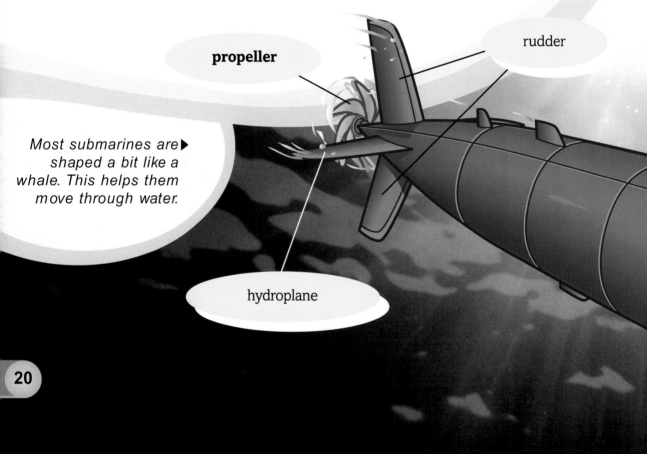

propeller

rudder

Most submarines are ▶ shaped a bit like a whale. This helps them move through water.

hydroplane

rudder blade at the back of a submarine

Keeping trim

The submarine must only tilt when the crew wants it to.
The weight of everything inside has to be balanced.
If one end is too heavy, the submarine tips like a seesaw.

Crew members check that each end of the submarine is
the same weight. This is called keeping "trim." There are
special trim tanks at each end of the submarine. The trim
tanks balance the weight of the submarine.

fin (conning tower)

hydroplane

Enemy in Sight

Wartime submarines had a fin on top. It was called the conning tower. It was packed with **instruments**. Instruments are tools and machines that help the crew. They can help crew members to **navigate**. Navigating means finding their way around.

Periscope up!

The **periscope** is used when the submarine is underwater. It lets crew members see what is happening on the surface. Periscopes are used to spy on enemy ships.

Crew members watch until the enemy gets close. Then, they launch a surprise attack with **torpedoes**. A torpedo is a weapon that can be fired underwater.

Radio messages

The conning tower had a mast to pick up radio messages. On the surface, crew members used the radio to talk to friendly ships. But it was dangerous to use the radio if enemy ships were nearby. The enemy ships might pick up the messages.

instruments	tools and machines that help the crew
navigate	find the way to a certain place
periscope	long tube lined with mirrors and lenses

▼ Periscopes are used before a submarine surfaces. Crew members check for enemy ships. They also check for icebergs.

23

Life in a Metal Tube

Life on board a wartime submarine was hard. Many sailors were packed into the small inner **hull**. They shared the space with large machines. **Torpedoes** and food were stored there, too.

The crew members often worked and slept in the same cramped room. Sailors usually wore the same clothes for the whole **voyage**. They hardly ever washed. Soap does not work in seawater. All the fresh water was saved for drinking.

There were no refrigerators on board. Fresh food only lasted a few days. Sailors ate canned and dried food for the rest of the trip. Most meals were cold. The battery power was too valuable to waste on cooking.

The air on board was damp and stale. Everything smelled. It smelled of unwashed feet, diesel fumes, and rotten food.

Bad smells!

Submarines were nicknamed "sewer pipes" and "pig boats" because they smelled so bad.

voyage journey at sea

25

▲ *Each man shared a small bed with several crewmates. They took turns sleeping.*

Super Submarines

Today's submarines are very different from wartime submarines. Many new submarines do not have a **diesel engine**. They use a different type of power.

These submarines only need new **fuel** every few years. Their engines do not need air to run. They can stay underwater for months at a time.

Crew members train to live at sea for a long time. They might not come to the surface for 70 days! Machines make drinking water. They take the salt out of seawater. Air conditioning units make fresh air for the crew to breathe.

Modern submarines are larger than wartime submarines. They are also faster. But they dive in the same way. The submarine's **ballast tanks** are filled with water. This increases its weight (pulling down). It is now greater than the **buoyant force** that pushes it up. The submarine sinks.

Modern submarines have more ▶ room for crew members to exercise. They also have exercise equipment to help the crew stay fit.

Inside a Submarine

Could you cope with life as part of a submarine crew? This is a cut-away picture of a diesel submarine. It shows how cramped it is to live underwater.

FACT LOG
for the modern diesel Canadian submarine HMS *Windsor*

Number of crew:
53

Length:
230 feet (70.3 meters)

Height:
25 feet (7.6 meters)

Width:
18 feet (5.5 meters)

Deepest dive:
656 feet (200 meters)

Top speed underwater:
More than 28 miles per hour (45 kilometers per hour)

Top speed on the surface:
More than 14 miles per hour (22 kilometers per hour)

Weapons:
18 **torpedoes**

propeller

trim tank

engine room

galley (kitchen)

head (toilets)

weapons store

control room

officers' quarters

ballast tank

mess deck
(dining room)

bunks

Glossary

ballast tanks big tanks inside a submarine that can be empty or full of water

buoyant force force that pushes an object upward when it is in water

compressed crushed into a small space. Submarines carry compressed air to fill the ballast tanks.

density mass of an object divided by its size

diesel engine machine that burns diesel fuel to release energy. On a submarine, this energy is used to turn the propeller. It also recharges the submarine's batteries.

displace move out of the way. Water is displaced by any object put into it.

electric engine machine that releases energy from electricity. An electric engine turns a submarine's propeller while the submarine is underwater.

expand spread out to fill more space. Gases, such as air, expand when they are let into a larger space.

force push or pull. Forces can change the movement or shape of an object.

fuel anything that is burned to release energy

gravity force that pulls everything toward the center of Earth

hollow has an empty space inside

hull metal body of a submarine. The hull of a submarine has two layers. The crew lives inside the inner hull.

instruments tools and machines that help the crew

lookout sailor looking out for enemy ships

mass how much there is of an object

navigate find the way to a certain place

periscope long tube lined with mirrors and lenses. One end of the tube sticks out of the water. Sailors can see what is happening on the surface.

propeller spinning blades that push a submarine through water

rudder blade at the back of a submarine. The rudder moves from side to side to steer the submarine.

torpedo weapon that can be fired underwater. Torpedoes are shaped like rockets.

voyage journey at sea

Want to Know More?

Books to read

- Hareas, John, and Neil Mallard. *Submarine*. New York: DK, 2003.
- Kramer, Sydelle. *Submarines*. New York: Random House Books for Young Readers, 2005.
- Stewart, Melissa. *Will It Float or Sink?* New York: Children's Press, 2006.

Websites

- http://www.pbs.org/wgbh/nova/subsecrets/inside.html

  Take an exciting online tour inside a wartime submarine.

- http://www.ed.gov/pubs/parents/Science/floats.html

  This experiment will help you to understand why things float or sink.

- http://www.ussnautilus.org/

  Visit the U.S. Navy Submarine Force Museum website to find out more about past and future submarines.

You may not think so, but it is possible to escape gravity. To find out how, read *10 Experiments Your Teacher Never Told You About*.

The Extreme Zone explores the forces used by those who take part in the world's most extreme sports.

Index